At the Top of Their Game

Simone Biles

Dominant Gymnast

Bethany Bryan

Cavendish Square
New York

Published in 2020 by Cavendish Square Publishing, LLC
243 5th Avenue, Suite 136, New York, NY 10016

First Edition

Website: cavendishsq.com

Library of Congress Cataloging-in-Publication Data

Names: Bryan, Bethany, author.
Title: Simone Biles : dominant gymnast / Bethany Bryan.
Description: First edition. | New York : Cavendish Square, 2020. | Series: At the top of their game | Audience: Grades: 9-12. | Includes bibliographical references and index.
Identifiers: LCCN 2019010878 (print) | LCCN 2019014663 (ebook) | ISBN 9781502651112 (ebook) | ISBN 9781502651105 (library bound) | ISBN 9781502651082 (pbk.) | ISBN 9781502651099 (6 pack)
Subjects: LCSH: Biles, Simone, 1997---Juvenile literature. | Women gymnasts--United States--Biography--Juvenile literature.
Classification: LCC GV460.2.B55 (ebook) | LCC GV460.2.B55 B79 2020 (print) | DDC 796.44092 [B] --dc23
LC record available at https://lccn.loc.gov/2019010878

Editor: Jodyanne Benson
Copy Editor: Michele Suchomel-Casey
Associate Art Director: Alan Sliwinski
Designer: Joe Parenteau
Production Coordinator: Karol Szymczuk
Photo Research: J8 Media

The photographs in this book are used by permission and through the courtesy of: Cover Francois Nel/Getty Images; p. 4 lazyllama/Shutterstock.com; pp. 6-7, 20-21, 80 Kyodo News/Getty Images; p. 10 John Lamparski/Getty Images; p. 14 Cal Sport Media/AP Images; p. 16 Michele Oenbrink/Alamy Stock Photo; p. 18 CasarsaGuru/E+/Getty Images; pp. 24, 28, 32-33, 46-47, 60, 64, 85 ©AP Images; p. 36 The Asahi Shimbun/Getty Images; pp. 38-39, 74-75 Colorado Springs Gazette/Tribune News Service/Getty Images; p. 42 Tim Clayton/Corbis Sport/Getty Images; pp. 50-51 Christopher Morris/Corbis Sport/Getty Images; p. 54 Manny Millan/Sports Illustrated/Getty Images; p. 57 Donna Ward/Getty Images; p. 62 Sean M. Haffey/Getty Images; pp. 68-69 AAron Ontiveroz/The Denver Post/Getty Images; p. 72 Robert Beck/Sports Illustrated/Getty Images; p. 82 Bill Smith/National Hockey League/Getty Images; p. 88 David Livingston/Getty Images; p. 94 The Boston Globe/Getty Images.

Printed in the United States of America

At the Top of Their Game

Contents

OLYMPICS
2016

Introduction

Four-Foot-Eight Powerhouse

Standing back-to-back with Olympic men's volleyball team center David Lee, gymnast Simone Biles grinned for a photo opportunity—better known as a photo op—during the 2016 Olympic Games. At just 4 feet 8 inches (1.4 meters) tall, Biles stands 2 feet (0.6 m) shorter than Lee. The top of her head barely reaches the middle of Lee's back, but the smile on her face said she didn't mind. "Size difference in Olympians doesn't matter," said Biles when she posted the photo on Twitter. Of the 555 athletes who made up the American team in 2016, Biles was the shortest. However, the four-time all-around world champion went home with a record-breaking four gold medals. Today, she is one of the most decorated athletes in the world—between the World Championships and the Olympics, she has twenty-five total medals as of summer 2019.

Competitive Gymnastics

Gymnastics is often argued to be one of the most difficult sports

Opposite: Simone Biles and the other members of the US women's gymnastics team made their mark on the sport, winning team gold to follow up the 2012 team win.

in the world. It combines grace with high levels of athleticism. Gymnasts strive for perfect scores, performing gravity-defying stunts such as those done on the balance beam, which measures only 4 inches (10 centimeters) in width. This requires a great deal of core strength, balance, concentration, and practice. The main competition events for women's gymnastics—the balance beam, the vault, the floor exercise, and the uneven bars—require athletes to stick the landing, or land solidly on their feet without a slip or extra hop. The tiniest mistake could cost a gymnast a medal, her career, or even her life. Injuries happen often and are sometimes expected.

Professional female gymnasts often retire from the sport in their late teens or early twenties because of the physical strain the sport places on their bodies. Gold medalist Mary Lou Retton retired in 1986 at eighteen. In her

Simone Biles's best event is the floor routine. Here, she shines in a floor routine performance that would win her a gold medal at the 2016 Olympics.

thirties, Retton had two hip replacement surgeries to ease arthritis pain caused by years of gymnastics. Carly Patterson, who competed in Athens in 2004, also retired at eighteen because of back problems. Jordyn Wieber, 2012 Olympian, retired at nineteen. Competitive gymnasts train for several hours each day, adding up to over thirty hours a week at certain competition levels, in addition to time spent in school, completing homework, or even just helping out with chores at home. Being a competitive gymnast is a lifestyle and a choice that often requires a sacrifice of friendships, normalcy, and a sense of personal identity.

Additionally, gymnastics is getting more difficult. The sport is scored currently on a basis of difficulty. Difficult routines are automatically scored higher than simpler ones, so gymnasts push themselves to perform increasingly difficult stunts, raising the bar on what an athlete needs to do to compete and ultimately medal in competition.

Standing Out from the Rest

Simone Biles stands out among her peers because she pushes the boundaries of what the human body can do. She sets the bar for difficulty levels in the sport. She can launch herself over 9 feet (2.7 m) into the air—over twice her height. In her floor exercise routine, Biles frequently performs a double half layout with a full twist, sticking a blind landing—one where the gymnast cannot see the floor before she hits the mat. This move is so iconic to Biles that it's called the "Biles" when it's seen in gymnastics competitions. She's one of the only athletes to even try it.

However, Simone Biles wasn't born a gymnast. She endured early family hardship and uncertainty before finding her way into her chosen sport. Gymnastics came naturally to her, but she trained hard for her success. Biles also stands out as an African American woman in a sport historically dominated by white gymnasts. Because of this, many argue that she is held to a higher standard, especially when it comes to her appearance.

In 2017, she faced criticism over her hairstyle during an appearance to cheer at a Houston Texans football game. However, Biles is outspoken, body positive, and defiant of her critics. In response to the comments over her hair, she replied, via Twitter, "I have 1 question to everyone commenting about my hair when I genuinely look happy in the photo.. Do you look perfect ALL the time? everything in perfect order.?" Simone Biles stands up for what she believes in.

In 2018, then president and CEO of USA Gymnastics Mary Bono tweeted a photo of herself coloring over the Nike swish on her shoes, in defiance of Nike's new advertising campaign featuring Colin Kaepernick, who famously chose to take a knee during the playing of the national anthem to protest police brutality and racism. Biles, who is sponsored by Nike, quickly spoke out against the tweet. Bono resigned shortly thereafter.

Simone Biles is redefining gymnastics. She shows no signs of slowing down and is working to create positive change within her sport, all the while training hard for her next competition.

ES & NOBLE
BN.co

Chapter 1

Unconventional Family

Simone Arianne Biles was born on March 14, 1997, in Columbus, Ohio. Her birth mother's name is Shanon, and when Simone was born, she had two older siblings: her sister, Ashley, and her brother, Tevin. Two years later, her younger sister, Adria, came into the world. Life was hard for Simone and her siblings when they were small. Simone's father wasn't around anymore, and Shanon had issues with drug and alcohol addiction and was often neglectful. Some of Simone's earliest memories are of feeling hungry and upset, she mentions in her 2016 autobiography, titled *Courage to Soar*. When Simone was three, some neighbors called child protective services, and the siblings went to live with a foster family for a while. This would hopefully give Shanon a chance to recover from her addictions and work on preparing to be a better mom, while the children lived in a more comfortable and safe environment.

The foster family had a big backyard with lots of space to run and play. In addition to Simone and her siblings, the foster parents

Opposite: Simone Biles signs copies of her 2016 autobiography, *Courage to Soar*, in which she talks about how she became an award-winning gymnast.

had children of their own, so the yard was frequently buzzing with activity. Simone was feisty and fearless. She loved to run, and she was fast. Anything her siblings did, Simone wanted to do, too. When Tevin would swing high into the air on the swing set and then do a backflip down to the ground, Simone wasn't about to let her older brother hog the spotlight. She flipped out of the swing right alongside him. The only thing the siblings weren't allowed to do was jump on the family's trampoline because their foster parents were afraid they would get hurt, especially little Simone. Simone and her siblings could only watch as the older children played on the trampoline. Simone longed to bounce and flip high into the air. Little did she know that she would one day get to do just that.

Ashley and Tevin and Simone and Adria

Simone, Tevin, Ashley, and Adria had been in foster care for a few months when their grandpa came for a visit. Ron Biles and his wife, Nellie, lived in Texas. Shanon was Ron's daughter from his first marriage, and after he heard that the children were in foster care, he began working with lawyers to get custody of his grandchildren. Nellie was a little more reluctant to add four additional children to their family. Ron and Nellie still had kids of their own at home, teenage sons Ron Jr. and Adam. Six kids under one roof would mean a lot more responsibility and putting off any travel plans until after their sons left home. Nellie decided that the best thing to do was pray and see what God wanted her to do. She was at work one day when she met a woman who had adopted a child with special needs. The woman had felt some of the same concerns that Nellie was feeling, mostly that she wasn't strong enough for the task ahead. The woman told Nellie her story and then comforted her by saying that God never gives you more than you can handle. On her way home that night, Nellie thought about that conversation. She wondered if the woman was a guardian angel, sent to tell her what to do. When she got home, she knew that she and Ron had to bring Ashley, Tevin, Simone, and Adria home to live with them.

The day after Ron arrived in Ohio, Simone boarded a plane for the very first time, and she and her siblings were on their way home to Texas.

A Home in Texas

Simone could barely contain her excitement upon arriving at Ron and Nellie's home in Spring, Texas, a Houston suburb. She dashed from the car and into the house to check out the room she would share with Ashley and Adria. There was a shelf full of Junie B. Jones and Cinderella books. Simone was over the moon! Her amazing new bedroom paled in comparison, though, to what Simone spotted in the backyard: a trampoline. Nellie told her she was welcome to use it. Simone could not get downstairs and out the door fast enough.

About eight months after the children moved to Texas, Shanon came for a visit. While Ashley and Tevin ran to hug their mom, Simone stood back, feeling apprehensive. Even at three years old, she had felt a sense of normalcy and comfort in Texas, and she worried that Shanon's visit would disrupt her life again. She was beginning to accept Ron and Nellie as solid parental figures in her life, but it was apparent that Tevin and Ashley longed to move back to Ohio again. The social worker overseeing their case recommended keeping the family together, so Simone and her siblings headed back to Ohio. Before long, though, Shanon began to show signs that she was

Nellie Biles (*left*) is Simone's adopted mom, but Simone has called her "Mom" since she was six years old.

struggling with addiction again. This time, child services intervened more aggressively, and the children were put up for adoption. Although Ron and Nellie wanted to keep all of the kids together and bring them back to Texas, Tevin and Ashley longed to stay close to Shanon. In the end, Simone and Adria moved to Texas permanently, while their older siblings were adopted by their Aunt Harriet in Cleveland and stayed behind.

In 2003, Ron and Nellie officially adopted Simone and Adria. Simone was six, and Adria was four. After the adoption, Simone began to call Nellie and Ron "Mom and Dad." They've been her parents ever since.

With two new older brothers, Simone learned a lot. Adam especially liked to drive Simone and Adria to school, putting on James Brown's "Say It Loud, I'm Black and I'm Proud" in the car and turning it way up so the girls would shout "I'm black and I'm proud!" The song instilled in Simone a sense of pride in her black culture. Most of the children Simone went to school with were white, but Simone held fast to her heritage. She felt that being black made her unique and special.

Nellie Biles is from the Central American country of Belize, bordering Guatemala and just south of Mexico's Yucatán Peninsula. Belize was once the home of a number of ancient Maya cities, including Cahal Pech, a vast, beautiful city that is now a ruin under archaeological study and a tourist destination. Nellie's love of her home country soon trickled down to Simone, especially when Nellie's mom, Everista Cayetano (Grandma Caye) moved to the United States to live with the family during the last few months of her life. A big part of Belizean culture is caring for family, and Simone was witness to this from an early age. She began to

Nellie Biles is from Belize. This Central American country has hundreds of Maya sites, including Cahal Pech, a city that is now a ruin.

understand that this was why Nellie felt so strongly about being a good mother to Simone and her siblings. Family was important! Even today, Simone Biles feels strong ties to Belize and even has dual citizenship through her mother.

Simone was also raised with strong religious values that tie back to her Belizean heritage. As children, after Grandma Caye passed away, Simone and her sister Adria would hang out in the bathtub and sing hymns from their grandma's funeral program. They felt that singing a hymn helped them to keep her in their hearts. Today, Simone continues to identify as a Catholic and often prays for comfort in times of need—especially before a competition. She mentions in her 2016 book that one of her greatest accomplishments was her confirmation, which is meant to seal a baptized person with the gift of the Holy Spirit.

Simone Finds Her Passion

Even as she continued to grow, Simone Biles remained small, smaller than everyone around her. It was because of this that she grew up with a drive to try to prove she was as good as everyone else. "If someone told me to do five push-ups, I'd do ten," she said in *Courage to Soar*. As with imitating Tevin as he performed stunts on the swing set long ago, Simone would pick things up after watching someone else do them and then insist on trying them herself. She was also stubborn and refused to give up if she didn't do something right the first time. As it turns out, these instincts were a perfect segue into gymnastics.

When Simone was six, she and the other children at her day care were supposed to take a field trip to a farm. However, it rained that day, so rather than disappointing the kids, the day care teachers—

This sight is a common one for many artistic gymnasts who train daily in their sport. A gym where gymnasts train often has equipment for every gymnastics event for men and women.

including Simone's big brother Adam, who worked part-time there while he went to school—came up with a backup plan. Adam suggested taking the children to Bannon's Gymnastix, just down the street from the day care and perfect for a high-energy group of kids.

At Bannon's, Simone was enchanted by what she saw. There was gym equipment everywhere, and some of it was just her size! Simone watched as a young gymnast performed a back handspring on the vault, and she couldn't wait to try the move herself. Adam saw Simone's excitement and challenged her to do a flip. She insisted that he try it first, and when Adam tried and fell, Simone knew she could do better. She did the backflip and added a little twist on the layout just for fun. She landed on her feet.

Simone's natural talent, energy, and enthusiasm had not gone unnoticed that day at Bannon's. When she landed her first backflip, one of the gymnastics coaches, Ronnie, came over to introduce herself and ask Adam if Simone wanted to sign up for a recreational gymnastics class. While Ronnie and Adam chatted, Simone continued to practice her flips, again and again, into the soft landing space of the gym's foam pit. Ronnie kept a close eye, giving Simone tips on improving her technique.

Later, at home, Simone begged her mother to let her take classes. Nellie saw an opportunity to find a fun activity for nonstop, high-energy Simone and agreed to sign her up, along with Adria, who was less enthusiastic about gymnastics than her sister. Nellie bought Simone and Adria brand-new leotards—the most important piece of apparel for a gymnast—from the Bannon's store. In their fashionable new outfits, the sisters were ready to hit the mat.

From day one, Simone was special. During her first class, Ronnie took a break from teaching to go find her daughter, Aimee Boorman.

Simone Biles performs a stellar balance beam routine in 2013, winning her first all-around gold medal at the World Championships.

She was the Bannon's coach who taught gymnasts who were older than Simone.

Aimee was impressed with what she saw, too. Simone had amazing upper-body strength for a six-year-old. In fact, at a gymnastics event not long after she started training, Simone climbed a rope using only her arms. The gymnasts were only required to get to about 10 feet (3 m), but Simone just kept climbing. Only when she was about 20 feet (6 m) in the air did she look down and notice that everyone was frantically trying to get her to come down.

Later, Simone did an impressive vault, fearlessly propelling herself into the air, much farther than the other gymnasts. After that, the coaches moved Simone up a level. They began training Simone on level five techniques. Then, they started preparing her for her first competition.

As a gymnast begins to learn and perfect her craft, she is subject to gymnastics levels developed by the Junior Olympic (JO) program. This program helps determine how prepared a gymnast is for competition. Levels one through three are learning levels, and these gymnasts do not compete in meets. However, they are required to master some of the basics of the vault, uneven bars, floor routine, and balance beam.

There are also age levels involved so that younger gymnasts do not get injured trying to master an advanced skill too soon. At levels four and five, gymnasts begin to compete in meets. To continue to level up as part of the Junior Olympic program, gymnasts must achieve a high score or place well in competition. It is not easy to get to a higher level.

Simone was a visual learner. She simply imitated what she saw. For instance, at seven, Simone watched one of the cheerleaders who also trained at the gym perform a standing back tuck, a challenging skill. "I can do that," she said to Aimee, who was standing nearby.

One of the other coaches teased Simone, betting her that she couldn't do it on the high beam—a level seven or eight skill. Simone ran to try, not realizing the coach was joking. Seeing that she had taken them seriously, the coaches ran to stop her before she could hurt herself.

Then, they moved her down to the floor beam. The floor beam is a practice beam that lies on the floor to help prepare gymnasts to move up to the balance beam. Simone did a standing back tuck on the floor beam on her very first try. Aimee told Simone later that this was the moment that she realized her student had the potential to be one of the greatest gymnasts in the world.

USA
VTB
USA

Chapter 2

Serious Competition

Lower-level gymnasts might spend a few hours at the gym each week. As they level up, they require more training and more hours to do it. Some elite gymnasts—those who have surpassed level ten—train thirty-five hours a week or more. Starting around level seven, gymnasts and their coaches begin to determine what's next. Is a gymnast physically capable of continuing to level up? Is she willing to dedicate extra time to training? Can she financially continue onward? (Gymnastics training can get very expensive, as private coaching becomes necessary.) Once a gymnast passes level ten—and few gymnasts do—they are considered an elite gymnast, with the goal of getting into a college gymnastics program or preparing for international competitions, like the Olympics.

Simone Biles worked her way upward through the levels quickly, training and participating in meets that grew more competitive as she continued to level up. However, every level comes with its own set of struggles, and although she was a natural, Simone faced many new challenges along the way.

Opposite: Simone strikes a warm-up pose at the World Artistic Gymnastics Championships in 2015.

Simone Levels Up

Learning how to do giants is a big deal in gymnastics. This is when a gymnast rotates 360 degrees around one of the uneven bars—usually the high bar, but shorter gymnasts can perform giants around the low bar—with her body fully extended. Giants are a level seven maneuver, and a gymnast must master them and then take the level seven test to move up from level six. If there was one thing that Simone Biles felt apprehensive about in her level six training, it was the high bar. The high bar is placed approximately 8 feet (2.4 meters) off the mat, so it was really high up for someone who stood under 5 feet (1.5 m) tall. Simone also had small hands, and hands are the most powerful tool on the uneven bars. The apparatus requires a certain level of control, too. Simone, however, was a "power gymnast," one who can fly high and perform powerful stunts but struggles when power isn't the top requirement.

As a level six gymnast, Simone was training with Bannon's coach Nicole, who pushed her hard on the uneven bars, often outside of her comfort zone. One time, as Simone attempted a giant, her hand slipped, and she bounced off the high bar, missed the mat, and landed on the concrete floor. She wasn't terribly hurt, but she was scared to try the move again. Coach Nicole insisted that she not only wanted Simone to hop right up and get back on that high bar, but she also wanted Simone to perform giants by the end of their training session that day. Simone wasn't used to Nicole's tough-love coaching technique, so she was mad and upset as Nicole lifted her back up to the bar and made her try again. However, as she swung into the air and felt that her body was in control, she felt her confidence returning. Shortly thereafter, although she had to take the test twice, Simone performed her giants and became a level seven gymnast. At this point, Aimee Boorman would take over coaching Simone, and their partnership would last the next eleven years.

A Career Taking Flight

Simone was now spending three to four hours at the gym after school every night. She was pushing the limits of her abilities on the floor routine, balance beam, and vault all the time. However, she was still struggling on the uneven bars, and Aimee pushed her harder to build her skills and confidence. In order to become a level eight gymnast, Simone was going to need to learn how to do a counter swing, or straddle back, in which the gymnast launches herself backwards in a straddle off the high bar and catches the low bar in a handstand position. This requires the gymnast to look back at the low bar in order to catch it, and what scared Simone most was looking for the low bar. It was really far away! Simone finally suggested to Aimee that she might quit bars altogether and specialize in only three events. This wasn't unheard of, just rare. Some gymnasts only master certain events. Simone had read about a gymnast named Alicia Sacramone who had quit bars, but Aimee refused to let Simone give up. "You have the ability to go as far as you can dream, Simone," she reminded her. Simone practiced on the bars so much that she started to dream about them. At last, practicing until the move became second nature, she mastered the counter swing and was able to level up. Other coaches advised Aimee that letting Simone level up too quickly would lead to burnout—an issue that lots of gymnasts deal with when they push themselves too hard—but Simone was tireless and loved competing.

Coach Aimee

Once a teen gymnast herself, Aimee Boorman (*right*) saw talent in Simone Biles from the start and coached her for many years.

At the age of fourteen, then a level eight gymnast herself, Aimee Boorman broke her leg, and the injury was so severe that she knew her gymnastics career was over. It was then that she made the choice to stop training and competing as a gymnast herself and start coaching instead. (Many gymnastics coaches start out as teenagers.) Then, she met six-year-old Simone Biles. One thing that made Aimee a good coach for Simone was that she knew when to push her student to work harder and when to step back and let her push herself.

As Simone leveled up past Aimee's own experience levels, the two had to learn together to help Simone master new skills. Aimee had never trained an elite gymnast before, and soon, the Biles family needed to decide whether to leave Simone's training in Aimee's hands or find her a more elite coach. In all their years of training together, Simone and Aimee had developed a bond. Aimee knew that it would be a challenge to continue, but she felt confident. Still, she left the decision to Simone and her family because she wanted Simone to have the best coach possible. In the end, the Biles family chose to stay with Aimee. Shortly after the 2016 Olympics and Simone's success there, Aimee Boorman made the decision to accept a position as women's gymnastics director at a Florida gym and moved on from being Simone's coach. Although their partnership ended, the two remain close.

Aimee, Ron, and Nellie let Simone use her own judgment when it came to pushing herself along. She had her heart set on eventually joining the national team.

Simone Biles became a level nine gymnast at the age of eleven when she was in sixth grade. There were only two gymnasts at that level at Bannon's at the time. She was also starting to win regularly at meets.

In early 2008, Simone was preparing for the level nine Western Championships, which would take place in Kettering, Ohio. This competition was extremely significant because lots of very important people from the world of gymnastics would be there, including national team coordinator Martha Karolyi, whose name was synonymous with greatness.

Bela and Martha Karolyi were once the most celebrated gymnastics coaches in the world. They first rose to prominence, with Bela dominating the spotlight, when one of their early students, Nadia Comăneci of Romania, scored the very first perfect ten in Olympic gymnastics history, at Montreal in 1976. She also won gold in the all-around competition—the youngest gymnast in history to do so. Her success, and the Karolyis' success, made then-communist Romania the country to beat in international competition. In 1981, the Karolyis defected from Romania—left their country to seek refuge in another nation—and settled in the United States, where they took over coaching the United States gymnastics team. The United States had never dominated in gymnastics, but the Karolyis would change all that. Under their tutelage, Mary Lou Retton won five gold medals in the 1984 Olympic Games. The Karolyis also led the 1996 team, known as the Magnificent Seven, to victory. After the Karolyis took over coaching the United States Olympic team, the

United States became known as a gymnastics powerhouse. Getting a spot at their training camp in Huntsville, Texas, was the dream of many gymnasts.

Simone performed well at the competition, but it would be a while yet before Martha Karolyi would invite her to train at their camp. Martha selected only the very best, and Simone wasn't quite ready.

Bumps in the Road

In order to compete in the Olympics, a gymnast must be at least sixteen years old. Simone knew this, but it didn't stop her from daydreaming about competing in the 2012 Olympics in London; she would only be fifteen and thus ineligible until 2016. Waiting is hard for a gymnast, and waiting meant four extra years of risking an injury that could end her career. Simone would be nineteen years old in 2016, retirement age for many gymnasts.

Simone continued to train, determined to get to the Olympics in 2016. She had finally become a level ten gymnast and was beginning to compete at that level. In 2010, she competed at the Houston National Invitational, placing first in vault and floor exercise—against 685 other gymnasts! This win came with a cash prize of $5,000, but Simone knew she couldn't accept the money. If she did, it would make her ineligible for college gymnastics. The prize was accepted by Simone's gym instead.

After this competition, Aimee decided to send a video recording of Simone's performance to Martha Karolyi. The feedback that came in from Karolyi was disappointing. "This kid has no bars," she said and refused to give Simone an invitation to training camp.

Longtime US gymnastics coaches Bela and Martha Karolyi were familiar faces for Olympic viewers and fans of the sport.

Additionally, Simone was struggling to balance school with spending extra time at the gym. The Biles family was getting ready to move. The new house was bigger (Simone and Adria would finally have their own bedrooms!) but this would mean changing schools and making all new friends. In addition, the gym was now farther away, and the family was struggling to find a solution to make things easier for Simone. Finally, they decided to enroll Simone in a private school right across from the gym. Then, she could get in a few hours of practice before school started each day. The school, however, was not Simone's favorite environment, and she struggled there. A young student who struggled with behavior issues tried to stab Simone with a pocketknife, and when she ran to the school office to complain, no one believed her. For a while, her only source of comfort was training as hard as she could at the gym.

A Shot at the National Team

The Gliders National Elite Qualifier took place in February 2011 in Riverside, California. Simone was feeling good in the time leading up to the competition. She had been pushing Aimee to let her increase the difficulty on some of her routines, which would hopefully increase her competition value among the other elite gymnasts. Simone felt this might be the meet that would finally get the attention of the Karolyis, if she performed well.

On her first vault, Simone landed with a little step. Her second vault needed to be flawless, and she and Aimee both knew it. As Simone launched herself into the round-off back handspring, she knew she would stick the landing—and she did. Her performance on the uneven bars was pretty simple, and she wobbled on the balance beam. However, with the vault and her floor routine—Simone's favorite and best event—she found herself in first place in the all-around competition, winning the gold medal at the event. This time, there was better news from Martha Karolyi. Simone had qualified for the American Classic, which was held at Karolyi Ranch. A good performance at that meet would guarantee Simone entry to the Visa National Championships later that year. Simone could go to Nationals! First, though, she would need to complete a five-day training session at Karolyi Ranch.

While other gymnasts had referred to the training period as "camp," it was as far from canoeing and arts and crafts as a camp can get. Every day, gymnasts trained from 8 a.m. to 7 p.m. under the watchful eye of coaches who specialized in each event—and they worked the gymnasts hard, striving for perfection. Simone was training alongside some of the best gymnasts in the United States, gymnasts she had read about in *USA Gymnastics* magazine. Martha Karolyi herself would walk through the gym and advise the coaches on each gymnast's form. There wasn't any room for goofing off at the ranch and absolutely no room for big errors.

While Simone was continuing to improve her skills on the uneven bars, one move was proving elusive: the Tkatchev. She needed to master it, and soon, to be ready for Nationals.

To perform the Tkatchev, a gymnast moves into a giant on the high bar, rotating 360 degrees around to gain speed, and then releases, flying backwards over the bar before catching it again. The Tkatchev is a common move today, but in the 1970s, when audience members saw Russian gymnast Alexander Tkachyov perform it the first time, they were amazed.

The Tkatchev requires extreme confidence and a level of

Alexander Tkachyov of the Soviet Union performs here on the horizontal bar apparatus, which only men compete on, in 1977.

fearlessness to let go of the high bar in midair and then catch it again, all while soaring backward. Simone kept missing the bar and falling to the mat during practice, and she was starting to feel like a failure. The American Classic competition was closing in.

The day finally arrived, and Simone was feeling overwhelmed going into the pre-competition warm-up. She hadn't caught the Tkatchev once in practice, and she was about to compete against some of the greatest gymnasts in America.

She was also totally starstruck. Just that morning, she had met Lexie Priessman, one of her gymnastics idols, and had barely said a word to her in her amazement. The stress of her failures during warm-up finally became too much, and Simone disappeared into the bathroom to cry. Suddenly, who should arrive in the very same bathroom but Lexie Priessman herself. Lexie saw Simone crying, and she came over to check on her. She understood Simone's predicament because she had also struggled with the Tkatchev. She explained to Simone that she needed to let go sooner, even if it seemed like it might be too soon.

Later, as Simone prepared to perform her routine on the uneven bars, she looked over to see Lexie giving her the thumbs-up. Her confidence returned. She took Lexie's advice and caught the Tkatchev! Simone was so surprised, though, that she fell twice on a few of her other moves. She was still excited and proud, though, and soon headed to Nationals, since she had placed third in the junior all-around.

Back to School

In school, Simone was facing some all-too-familiar challenges. She had always struggled with sitting in a classroom and paying

Simone Biles is what has become known as a power gymnast, or one who is compact and muscular and can soar high in the air, as she's shown doing here in 2016.

attention. Finally, Simone was tested for attention-deficit/hyperactivity disorder (ADHD), and she discovered the source of her issues with concentration and boundless energy. People often assume that with ADHD, people can't stay focused on anything, but actually, it can make a person very focused on certain things. For instance, an avid reader with ADHD might finish a book in one sitting but also struggle to sit still during a test. A gamer with ADHD might play a video game for hours but struggle to complete a simple homework assignment. For Simone, the target of her hyper-focus was gymnastics. She was tireless when it came to practicing one move over and over until she got it right.

Simone had been working so hard to perfect the Tkatchev that, going into Nationals, she felt great about her routine on the uneven bars. Her downfall in the competition would prove to be the Amanar instead, a vault maneuver that starts off with a back handspring going into a layout with two and a half twists.

The move is difficult, so this often results in a higher score if the gymnast can nail it. However, Simone wasn't feeling confident enough to try it in competition, so she chose a simpler vault. She finished the meet just one place away from qualifying for the junior National team. She was crushed.

After years of competing, though, Simone knew that the best thing to do is not let disappointment get you down. She just needed to work harder, and with Nationals out of the way, she and Aimee could spend time focusing on honing specific skills, like controlling her landings. Simone could launch herself high into the air, but she couldn't always stick her landings. As her freshman year of high school began, Simone was training twenty-five to thirty hours at the gym every week.

Simone was beginning to understand that she needed to make some hard decisions and make them soon. Staying in school meant seeing her friends every day and getting to act like a normal teenager. However, switching to being homeschooled would give her more time at the gym, but she would have to sacrifice time with friends and possibly feel a lot more isolated. Simone didn't know what to do because less time in training might mean a departure from elite gymnastics altogether. Ron and Nellie wanted Simone to make the decision on her own because they didn't want to sway her into feeling pressured one way or the other.

Finally, she realized that her friends were never really far away as long as social media and texting existed. They could still talk all the time. She also reminded herself of something her dad said once: "Simone, never squander what God has given you." In the end, Simone decided that it was time to focus on her training. Ron and Nellie hired a tutor, who Simone called Miss Heather, who had experience working with gymnasts. The Olympics were in Simone's future, and she needed to be ready.

Chapter 3

Four Years of Anticipation

At Bannon's, all eyes were on the television screen. It was 2012, and the "Fierce Five"—Jordyn Wieber, Kyla Ross, Aly Raisman, Gabby Douglas, and McKayla Maroney—were representing the United States at the Olympics in London. Gymnastics is a sport where, although gymnasts compete against each other, they're also teammates. Showing your support to a friend is important, even if they take home a medal and you don't. A win for the women's gymnastics team in London was a win for the sport of gymnastics. Hence, the Bannon's crew was sure to check in on their heroes and friends.

Back in 1996, the "Magnificent Seven"—Amanda Borden, Amy Chow, Dominique Dawes, Shannon Miller, Dominique Moceanu, Jaycie Phelps, and Kerri Strug—gave the United States its first team gold in women's gymnastics. As the competition wound down to the final days, the gymnasts themselves were all fighting pain from minor injuries, but Kerri Strug was very concerned about her ankle. The landing of her first vault on the final day of team competition

Opposite: When photographed in midair, it's easier to see the signs of extreme concentration on a gymnast's face.

had severed two of her ligaments. However, she knew she had to go on. Landing her second vault would give the American team the gold medal over Russia. The world held its breath as Kerri Strug dashed toward the vault. She went into a perfectly executed back handspring. On the landing, which she stuck perfectly, she heard a second crack. The pain was overwhelming, and Strug fell to the mat, but only after smiling at the judges to complete the routine. The American team had won the gold, thanks to Kerri Strug and her sheer grit, overcoming an injury to bring her team to victory. This win put a lot of expectation on future gymnastics teams. They had to be as excellent as the Magnificent Seven, better even, if the United States was going to continue to dominate the sport.

The Fierce Five felt this pressure to be excellent. The media had its expectations, and so did the Karolyis. The United States team had won the bronze in 2000, and this just wasn't good enough. Martha Karolyi believed that getting the team back to gold status would mean making a lot of changes. She wanted the team to have a certain chemistry and a sense of togetherness that the Magnificent Seven had enjoyed. This camaraderie appealed to viewers back home and made them root for the athletes through both their triumphs and failures. An Olympic athlete becomes a type of celebrity as different events are broadcast. Americans needed someone to root for, if they were going to tune in to watch. Gold medals brought good ratings and a high viewership for the NBC network. The small-statured, fiercely competitive women's gymnastics team always has viewer appeal, so their events are very important. The team needed to do well.

Going into the 2012 Olympics, the gymnasts had upped their difficulty levels in preparation for whatever was to come from the other teams. The strategy worked. People couldn't get enough of the Fierce Five. Gabby Douglas became the first African American gymnast to win the all-around competition. On the final day of competition, the American team was down to a difficult vault once again. McKayla Maroney needed to perform a nearly perfect Amanar if the women's gymnastics team would take the gold. Maroney was up to the challenge. Her vault was perfection. The American women's gymnastics team won the gold. Said Martha Karolyi of the win, "We are certainly enjoying this moment. This is the result of the teamwork and what we did through the years. All the hard work paid off in the end."

Back at Bannon's, Simone had chills. "That could be you, Simone!" one of the other gymnasts called out. Simone was touched by her friends' enthusiasm, but she knew that she could only focus on one competition at a time. A lot could happen in four years.

Building Momentum

Simone was improving all the time, and it was starting to really pay off. Going into the 2012 competition season, she was performing very well. When the American Classic competition rolled around again, this time Simone's Amanar was ready. She took first place on the vault. In fact, she placed first in vault at every competition that season. Simone felt confident that this time she was going to make the national women's junior team. The Visa National Championships took place in St. Louis, Missouri, that year. Simone landed her Amanar easily, taking first place in the vault. She had been afraid to compete against other gymnasts like Lexie Priessman and Katelyn Ohashi, who had become her friends. She worried that if she outperformed them, they would stop liking her. Simone

USA
20

Katelyn Ohashi, shown here in 2013, took the internet by storm in 2019 with her show-stopping, personality-driven viral performances as part of the UCLA gymnastics team.

finally realized that she simply had to do her best and give her friends the competition they deserved and hope for the same from them. In the all-around competition Lexie Priessman won the gold, Madison Desch won the silver, and Simone was excited to stand alongside them with the bronze medal around her neck. When the junior national team was announced, Simone's name was on the list.

Making the national team meant heading back to the Karolyis for camp in early 2013. The American Cup was coming up, and although Simone wasn't originally on the roster for it, two other gymnasts had suffered injuries and needed to be replaced. Martha Karolyi chose Katelyn Ohashi and Simone Biles. The American Cup was televised, and there would be a huge crowd. As competition day arrived, Simone was not feeling well. Her stomach hurt. Every move she tried brought her pain. Simone was afraid she was sick or injured.

Finally, seeing her distress, Martha Karolyi came over to check on her. The pain was just nerves, she reassured Simone. It happened to lots of gymnasts. Still, Simone knew that she had to perform well, especially in front of Martha, if she would ever be chosen for a task like this again.

Shaking off the nerves, Simone did well in her events. In fact, she was in first place as she got ready for the balance beam. During her double back-handspring, though, something went wrong. Simone fell off the beam, crashing to the floor. Horrified, she climbed back up and finished her routine, but with video cameras all around trying to capture her disappointment, Simone could barely keep her cool as she walked off the mat. The mistake itself was enough to cause her anguish, but what was Martha going to say?

The usually tough-as-nails Martha surprised Simone, though. She told her she was proud of her. Simone just needed to work harder on the beam to build her confidence.

Champion of the World

Simone Biles turned sixteen in 2013, moving her to the senior team roster. She was now competing at the highest level, but this didn't mean that she didn't make her fair share of mistakes. In July, she was scheduled to compete in the United States Secret Classic, but as the competition began, she couldn't stop making mistakes. She missed catching the Tkatchev—by then the maneuver was second nature, so Simone couldn't believe she'd messed up. Every event was a disaster, even the floor routine, Simone's specialty. On one tumbling pass, she landed poorly and hurt one of her ankles. Finally, Aimee decided to take Simone out of the competition. Worse, Martha wanted to talk to her. "This is what happens when you're not one hundred percent focused and trained and ready to do what you need to do," she said. Simone also overheard another coach comment that the reason she fell was because she was too fat. She knew she wasn't. She was shorter and more compact than some of the other athletes, making her appear more muscular. Still, the criticism hurt. She also knew that Martha was right: She hadn't been working hard enough to prepare for the meet. Ultimately, as she always did, she used her suffering as motivation. She worked harder than ever.

Simone also started to have regular visits with a sports psychologist to help her cope with the stress of pushing herself harder and harder toward her goals. Simone had always dealt with what she called "bratty periods," where things became too much and she started to act out. However, as a world-class gymnast, she couldn't afford to break down or stomp off in a huff. She needed to learn how to channel her frustrations into something useful. Through working with the psychologist, Simone realized that sometimes gymnastics just felt like work, when it used to feel like so much fun. She didn't perform well when she wasn't having fun. After this revelation, she was grateful for her poor performance at the United States Secret Classic. It helped to give her back her love of the sport. One thing that also helped Simone was showing up for other gymnasts and being supportive, no matter if they were teammates or opponents.

Simone was always watching other athletes perform and then offering them a high five, a hug, or a "Great job!" as they left the mat. It not only made the other athlete feel good, it was also Simone's

The Fierce Five team was made up of Jordyn Wieber, Gabby Douglas, McKayla Maroney, Aly Raisman, and Kyla Ross (*from left to right*).

London 2012
London 2012

way of mentally preparing for her own performance. However, this camaraderie wasn't going over well with Martha Karolyi. She wanted Simone to stay serious and focused and concentrate on preparing for her own routine. She believed that if Simone got distracted by the other athletes, she might not perform her best. Eventually, though, Martha came to realize that this was just "Simone being Simone." Simone was just being friendly and nice, and she liked to treat competition like an everyday practice at the gym so that she could go out and do her best without letting the nerves get to her. Finally, Martha accepted this part of Simone's personality and let her handle the stress in her own way.

Simone was feeling good again as the 2013 World Artistic Gymnastic Championships—or Worlds, for short—approached. She even got her parents to agree that they would let her get her belly button pierced if she won Worlds—a long shot in her parents' minds. The competition is a yearly event, and just getting selected for the six-woman team (or even as an alternate) is a huge deal. This international competition brings together the best gymnasts in the world.

On the first day of the competition, Simone decided on a specific strategy. Before she began an event, she would look for Martha. With Martha on her mind, Simone found it really hard to mess up. "Just do what you do in practice!" teammate Kyla Ross told Simone whenever she felt her nerves taking over. By the end, those words felt like a shared catchphrase between the girls.

Simone was still dealing with some pain from a calf injury she had sustained at an earlier competition, so she and Aimee had come up with a plan to help Simone do an incredible floor exercise with a high point value without risking further injury. The solution was a double layout with a half twist. In order to do it, Simone would have to learn how to stick the blind landing. She practiced the move until she had mastered it. When Simone stuck that move at Worlds, it became known henceforth as the Biles.

Simone had been in situations many times where performing well meant reaching the next step in her career as a gymnast. Sometimes, as in her first appearance in a national competition, things didn't go according to plan. This time, though—in front of an international crowd in Antwerp, Belgium, and with her family cheering her on—Simone performed like never before. She won the gold. The 2013 season was really looking up!

Simone Dominates

The next year at Worlds, Simone did it again, winning the gold medal and also charming gymnastics fans all over the world when, as she stood on the podium holding a bouquet of flowers, Romanian gymnast Lorisa Iordache pointed out that there was a bee in Simone's flowers. Simone panicked and tried to get away as the bee chased her. She was afraid to drop the flowers because it might offend the people of China, the host country that year. Finally, she dropped the bouquet, and the bee flew instead into the flowers bronze medalist Kyla Ross was holding. At last, the three medalists simply shared the top spot on the podium, as far from the bee as they could get, as they posed for photos with their medals.

The win was an important one for Simone because she had sat out much of the earlier part of the season due to a shoulder injury. Easing herself back into things, she had lowered the difficulty level of her routine on the uneven bars, taking out the Tkatchevs so that she didn't risk further injury by doing something too challenging.

Challenges for Black Gymnasts

There is a term used frequently in gymnastics journalism—the "Russian look"—that implies that white, thin, and graceful is the expectation for a female gymnast. The Soviet Union had long dominated the sport. Soviet gymnasts set the long-term standard with outward grace and hair pulled back tidily in a bun.

In 1996, Dominique Dawes was an important part of the Magnificent Seven.

Simone Biles—along with Betty Okino, Dominique Dawes, and Gabby Douglas before her—has redefined the sport. She's short and muscular. Her gymnastics style is driven by her strength. She pushes her body to higher levels of difficulty all the time. She is also an African American young woman in a sport that has often been dominated by white, European women.

Many people are bothered by a black woman dominating gymnastics, saying that they believe that a traditional, more graceful style should return, implying that power gymnasts lack grace. Many of these critics are simply deeply biased. After Simone won the gold at the 2013 Worlds, another gymnast, Carlotta Ferlito of Italy, who had finished in fifth place, made an offhand remark to the press that next time she and a teammate would "also paint our skin black so that we could win, too," implying that Simone was favored by the judges because of the color of her skin. Simone, though, brushed most of it off. Upon hearing Ferlito's comment (and subsequent apology), she tried not to let it get to her. She knew how it felt to be disappointed at the end of a meet and to say the wrong thing. Simone wasn't out there to please everyone. She wanted to be a good role model for the next generation and would simply continue to go out and do her best.

Even with the easier routine, Simone led the team with the highest execution score, and she felt good about that.

That same year, Coach Aimee decided to leave Bannon's, and she, Ron, and Nellie decided to go into business together, building a new gymnastics training center in Spring, Texas, called the World Champions Centre. The family hired new coaches, and the facility opened in 2015, becoming Simone's new gymnastics home.

That year also saw Simone Biles win her third consecutive gold medal at Worlds. This time, though, she was so worn out from training tirelessly in the time leading up to the competition that she could barely enjoy her win. Wanting only to go back to the hotel and climb into bed, she finally asked Aimee to confirm for her that she'd won.

The World Championship that comes before an Olympics year is important because it's one of the first qualifying rounds to determine who will join the Olympic team. The win almost guaranteed Simone a spot, if she could avoid injury for the next year and continue to perform well. Simone's dream of competing in the Olympics was closer than ever.

Simone Goes Professional

When Simone was thirteen and started to show enormous potential as a gymnast, college scouts had started to come around and watch her practice and compete. Acceptance into a college gymnastics program is highly competitive. It means getting a scholarship to a good college and getting an education that can lead to a career once a gymnast decides to retire. Lots of Simone's friends had headed off to college and loved it, and Simone liked to get lost in fantasies about team practices and enjoying time with her friends. She even had

With the decision to become a professional athlete, Simone Biles opened herself up to endorsements, like one with Nike.

her heart set on the University of California, Los Angeles (UCLA). This meant she would start college in 2016, unless she made the Olympic team, which would delay college for a year. However, with big wins at the international level, Simone had made a name for herself. She now had a second option: She could forego the college experience and turn professional.

Choosing to become a professional athlete is a big decision for an elite gymnast. Turning professional, or "pro," means accepting payments through prize money or endorsements. A basketball player or football player may see turning pro as a no-brainer because their sports are well funded through high attendance at games and advertising dollars.

When a gymnast goes pro, it means that they're no longer eligible to play college sports because college athletes are not paid—except through scholarship programs. This decision can be a big gamble because in order to be a successful professional athlete, you must have earning potential, attracting high-paying companies like Nike or Kellogg's. However, this earning potential goes down after an athlete retires. Meanwhile, a college gymnastics scholarship can help an athlete build a career after her time as a gymnast draws to a close.

Simone thought through the difficult decision. Going pro would mean financial security now. Choosing college would mean turning down millions of dollars in endorsements but having a relatively normal college experience among friends. Finally, Simone realized that she couldn't turn down the money. In late July 2015, Simone Biles made the decision to become a professional athlete. She and her parents hired an agent to help manage her career. They also decided to hire a financial advisor to help with her newfound fortune.

Soon, Simone was seeing some differences between being a pro athlete and being an amateur one. She was followed around by camera crews. People wanted interviews with her. She had responsibilities to her brand, so she knew she had to be nice and polite and let the good sides of her personality shine through, even when she wasn't in the mood to talk to people. A negative appearance could damage her earning potential.

As it turns out, going pro was a great choice for Simone Biles. Simone has a strong media presence and a lot of fans. People are charmed by her personality and her strong bond with her family. Many consider her a powerful role model for the next generation of athletes. This made her a great representative for companies like Hershey's, Nike, and Kellogg's. By the end of the 2016 Olympics, she was worth over $4 million in endorsements alone.

Huge Performances

The 2016 Pacific Rim Championships would take place in Everett, Washington, in early April. This would be the last big international gymnastics competition before the Olympics. The P&G National Championships were in June, and the Olympic trials would shortly follow that event. The next few months were crucial for Simone, and she needed to do a few important things. First, she needed to up her game. Other gymnasts were starting to realize that they had to increase the difficulty of their routines if they were going to beat Simone Biles, who had won eleven straight all-around titles since 2013. Simone had been dominating the vault with her flawless Amanar, but she knew she could push her difficulty level even more. She decided it was time to master the Cheng.

Cheng Fei of China performs a vault at the Beijing Olympics in 2008. Cheng's signature vault was called the "Cheng" in her name.

The Cheng is a layout front flip with one and a half twists, meaning that the gymnast does a layout onto the springboard, followed by a half turn onto the table. She then pushes off into a Rudi—a twist, or in this case, one and a half twists with the body fully extended—and lands facing the table again. Very few gymnasts even attempt the vault, which was first performed in competition by Chinese gymnast and extraordinary vault champion Cheng Fei in 2005.

Simone knew that the combination of her Amanar and the Cheng was what she needed to stay ahead of the competition. When she landed both vaults in competition, Simone looked over to see Martha giving her two thumbs up—a rare gesture from the coach. Next up was Nationals.

Martha Karolyi wanted her gymnasts to do well but not push themselves so hard they hurt themselves right before the Olympic trials, so she told them that it was fine to operate at only 90 percent. Simone had developed a skill where she could perform pretty consistently, almost like she was on autopilot, even when she was exhausted. The press had noticed it, too, sometimes referring to her as "the robot." Simone was exhausted going into Nationals. Despite a few missteps, she dominated again, walking away with the gold medal.

Finally, the Olympic trials were upon them. "It's unreal, actually, because we have been waiting so long for this," Simone said in an interview at the start of the event. This was the final event that would determine which athletes would be heading to Rio de Janeiro, Brazil, as part of the American team.

Olympic gymnastics hopefuls must show consistency in their routines over two days of events. Any elite gymnast can turn in a good performance or have a great practice, but they have to be able

Simone poses for a portrait at the 2016 Team USA Media Summit.

to shine it when it really counts—often in front of a huge, cheering crowd and a lot of cameras. This is very difficult. Simone often struggled in front of a packed stadium because the adrenaline took over. This made her lose some of her control. However, Simone also loved the energy of the crowd.

Simone had a rough start at the trials. She messed up on the uneven bars and made a mistake on the balance beam. Still, her two best events were yet to come: the vault and the floor routine. Simone gave it her all.

Her Amanar gave her a nearly perfect score. The only flaw was a tiny hop at the end. Simone ended up in first place. She, Gabby Douglas, Aly Raisman, Madison Kocian, and Laurie Hernandez were going to the Olympics.

USA

Chapter 4

The 2016 Olympic Games

Preparing for her first appearance in the Olympics, Simone asked Aly Raisman for her tips on avoiding nerves and doing her best. Raisman had won two gold medals in 2012, so she was a great sounding board for Simone's questions. "Go to bed early," she told Simone. "Remember to breathe." Her final tip: "Just don't look up at the Olympic rings."

Preparing to compete in the Olympics, Simone went into overdrive with her training. The five gymnasts who were going to Rio would be doing a special training camp at Karolyi Ranch, leaving from there for the Olympics. Leading up to that, Simone was spending extra time back at the World Champions Centre in Spring, Texas. Things were unfortunately not going Simone's way. The uneven bars at Rio were a different type of apparatus than Simone was used to, and the gym just had the new type installed to help her prepare. The Gymnova bars had a different feel. They were springier, and Simone felt herself flying faster on them. While this might seem like a good thing, gymnasts rely on feel and consistency

Opposite: As part of preparing for the Olympics, gymnastics hopefuls prior to 2016 would travel to Karolyi Ranch in Texas for extensive training. Simone is shown here training at the ranch.

in order to time a catch correctly. In that moment, Simone was feeling frustrated. Added in to that, she knew that the pressure was on after her first-place finish at the Olympic trials. She started to feel herself breaking down under the strain. One day when she was feeling especially frustrated, Aimee told her to just go home, get some rest, and come back the next day. Simone did. The next day, she felt better. She wasn't alone in her frustration over the bars. The other gymnasts were struggling to master them as well. They stayed in close contact via group text, and Simone could see that their messages sounded all too familiar.

Additionally, the team was struggling to pick an official name. It needed to be something good, unique, and memorable. This name is how the team would be remembered for generations to come, so it was no simple choice. The teammates didn't want it to be a cute or silly name, so they nixed "GLAM Squad" (representing each of their initials) pretty quickly. As they thought about the decision, they kept in mind that this Olympics would mark Martha Karolyi's final appearance as the women's team coach, as she was retiring. This was also the last time that each team would send five athletes. In 2020, the number would go down to four. The name they finally decided on seemed the most fitting. One last time, Martha Karolyi would coach a team of five gymnasts to victory. Their name: the Final Five.

The Final Five

The Final Five was made up of teammates Simone Biles, Aly Raisman, Laurie Hernandez, Gabby Douglas, and Madison Kocian. Raisman and Douglas had been part of the Fierce Five team that took home gold for the team competition in 2012 in London, so they would bring with them a heap of previous experience and leadership that would be helpful for the team. For Biles, Hernandez, and Kocian, this would be their first Olympics.

When putting together an Olympic gymnastics team, a coach has to consider each athlete's strengths and weaknesses. If one gymnast consistently has one event in which she struggles, then a coach is going to want to fill out the team with athletes who can make up for that weaker event. For example, Simone had always struggled at the uneven bars, but Gabby Douglas and Madison Kocian are considered two of the best at the event. They were both vital to the team's success. Everyone on a gymnastics team has a role to play. She has to look out for her own performance and be competitive, but she also has to be there for her teammates if the group wants to win the team event.

Another important consideration is finding someone to take on a leadership role within the team. Having coaches cheer you on is one thing, but a teammate who is out there giving her all, too, is going to make a huge difference to the team's morale. For the Final Five, that teammate was Aly Raisman. Raisman was elected team captain before both the 2012 and 2016 Olympics. Although her teammates teased her for her post-practice naps and being the oldest of all of them—resulting in the nickname "Grandma Aly"—they respected their leader. Aly had a way of telling them to be quiet, quit stressing, and get back out there. Her pep talks were sometimes just what they needed to get out of their own heads and back on the mat.

Although Gabby Douglas had struggled in the Olympic trials, ending up in seventh place, her skills on the uneven bars and her position as the defending gold medalist in the all-around made her a strong choice for the 2016 team.

The Final Five team included Simone Biles, Gabby Douglas, Laurie Hernandez, Madison Kocian, and Aly Raisman (*from left to right*). Here, they celebrate their team gold win at the 2016 Olympics.

Madison Kocian was the world champion in the uneven bars in 2015—she actually tied for first with three other gymnasts. Therefore, the team needed her to go out and perform well in the event they struggled with the most.

Laurie Hernandez was the youngest member of the Final Five, but what she lacked in age she made up for with an energetic floor routine. She turned in consistently amazing performances on the balance beam as well.

Of course, the Final Five was not complete without Simone Biles, who excelled at the floor routine, soared in her vaults, and claimed gold in three World Championships in a row. A lot of people were calling Simone the gymnast to beat at the 2016 Olympics, and they weren't wrong.

Ready for Rio

The Karolyis' training camp leading up to the Olympics lasted ten days. It was some of the hardest, most grueling training of Simone's life, but Aimee was there to help talk Simone through it. Of course, she would be there in Rio as well—a tough coach, but one who had believed in Simone long before she had met the Karolyis. In the few days before the teammates left for Rio, parents and family could come see them off and wish them well. "Promise me that you'll do your best," Nellie said during her visit to the camp. "This is your dream, Simone, so go out there and live it with everything you've got. And don't forget to have fun."

Ready or not, the last days flew by, a whirlwind of training, packing, and working through the jitters. On July 26, 2016, Simone Biles boarded a plane bound for Rio. For the first time in weeks, the team could enjoy a bit of a rest. Simone fell asleep and didn't wake up until they arrived in Brazil.

Arriving at the Olympics involves a lot of fanfare. There are photographers everywhere, along with fans seeking autographs. The Olympic Village, where the athletes live during the Olympics, is set up to give them everything they need to do well: lots of food, a pool, and living quarters that serve as their home for the duration of the event. Although there was a huge variety of food to choose from in the cafeteria, Simone and her teammates knew they couldn't go crazy and eat pizza and cheeseburgers all the time. Maintaining a healthy diet would help them perform at their best, so they had lots of steamed chicken, vegetables, and fruit instead.

There were also lots of familiar faces to see in the cafeteria. The team spotted British diver Tom Daley and US gold-medal swimmer Michael Phelps. However, it wasn't until they spotted Jamaican sprinter Usain Bolt that they almost lost their cool. "We're the gymnastics team," they said as they introduced themselves to Bolt at lunch one day. He said, smiling, "I can tell."

Simone shared a room in the team quarters with Laurie Hernandez. The two were a good pair and fast friends, both bubbly and enthusiastic and so excited to be in Rio. During what downtime the teammates had, they watched Netflix, listened to music, and hung out on the balcony of their living quarters, watching the other athletes work out below. However, they were there to do a job, and that job was to win gold—so it was off to the training center only an hour after they arrived in Rio.

Going for the Gold

The artistic gymnastics competition in the Olympics breaks down into four distinct parts: qualification round, team final, all-around, and individual events. Every country brings five gymnasts—changing to four gymnasts starting in 2020—and four out of five gymnasts from each team compete on each apparatus. The highest scores determine which eight teams will go on to the team final. Then, twenty-four gymnasts are selected to go on to the all-around final (only two can compete from each country). Finally, the eight gymnasts with the best scores on each apparatus move on to the individual events final. There is potential in the end for one gymnast to win six medals: for the balance beam, uneven bars, floor routine, vault, all-around, and team.

In the qualification rounds, the Final Five turned in incredible performances. Simone Biles landed both of her vaults with only a tiny hop at the end of one of them for an average score of 16.050. Aly Raisman also performed well with a score of 15.766 for both

Simone's coach, Aimee (*left*), was with her through the qualifying rounds at the 2016 Olympics and beyond.

vaults. Gabby Douglas achieved her best score of the season for her performance on the uneven bars. In the end, Simone Biles and Aly Raisman were selected as the two gymnasts to compete in the all-around. Simone also qualifed for the balance beam, floor exercise, and vault events. The American team left the qualifying round with a ten-point lead over China.

The team event came first, and the American team performed very well. They stuck every landing on the vault. Simone got the highest score on the balance beam, just edging out a competitor from the Netherlands, with Laurie Hernandez in a close third. Madison Kocian tied Aliya Mustafina of Russia for first on the uneven bars, with Gabby Douglas in second place.

It was in the floor routine that the team really soared. Biles, Raisman, and Hernandez placed first, second, and third, in a huge 3.234 first-place lead. Standing on the podium with her first gold medal around her neck, Simone couldn't help but feel so proud of herself and her teammates, but she was also all too aware that there were even more challenges to come.

The All-Around Competition

The all-around competition arrived two days later. Simone awoke to find only herself and Aly Raisman in the team apartment. The others had gone down to have breakfast since they weren't competing that day. The two friends got dressed together, with Simone putting on her favorite leotard, a sparkly red, white, and blue one. She had saved it for her performance in the all-around. Although they were competing against each other, they couldn't help but offer hugs and words of support to each other on the way down to the arena, leading up to the start of competition. The anticipation had made them both nervous.

Simone Biles flies high on the uneven bars during the 2016 Olympics. The hand grips she is wearing both keep her hands safe from blisters and help her grip the bar.

The vault came first. For this portion of the competition, gymnasts only perform one vault, and Simone and Aly were both planning to perform an Amanar. Each had a little hop on her landings, but the difficulty level of the vault helped them to start strong, leading the pack.

Next up was the uneven bars. Simone felt good, flying higher than ever on her Tkatchev and catching it easily. Her execution was flawless, but her final score was lower than expected because she had a decreased difficulty level at the start. This score would push uneven bars master Aliya Mustafina into first place at the end of that event.

However, the all-around competition was only halfway done. The third event was the balance beam. When Simone launched into her wolf turn and felt it go well, she knew she had the lead in her sights. The wolf turn is a traditional gymnastics move in which the gymnast spins around on one foot with the other foot extended. The announcer even called the turn "smooth as butter." Simone's confidence guided her through the rest of the routine and into a perfect dismount, a double twisting double tuck, one of the most difficult dismounts. The score came up 15.433—Simone was in the lead once again.

The floor routine came last. It was Simone's favorite event and the one in which she felt the most sure of herself. Still, she didn't want to go in to her performance feeling like she'd already won. She had to continue to perform her best. The familiar music of her routine began, and Simone felt her body take over. At the end of the performance, she looked up to see a 15.933 score. Simone had done it. She'd won gold in the all-around at the 2016 Olympics. Simone walked out onto the mat to wave at the crowd, but looking back over at her friend Aly Raisman, who had won the silver, she gestured to her friend to join her. The two waved at the crowd together to an overwhelming roar from the fans. In the stands, Ron, Nellie, and Adria stood cheering, hugging, and crying. Their girl had won the gold.

More Gold

In the individual events, Simone saw gold again. For the vault final, she would need to successfully perform two vaults. She performed her first vault, scoring a 15.900 for a well-executed Amanar. Her competitors for this event had pulled out all the stops to try to beat her. Dipa Karmakar of India had added an extremely difficult Produnova vault to her routine—one with a difficulty score of 7.0 (a Cheng is a score of 6.0). This vault is so difficult and so dangerous that many refer to it as the "vault of death." Simone Biles refuses to even perform it. "I'm not trying to die," she said once, in response to reporters wondering why she wasn't attempting the difficult maneuver. The so-called vault of death begins with the gymnast launching herself off the table into two and a half somersaults and then landing on both feet. One mistake in timing could paralyze a gymnast. Many who had tried the vault landed painfully, often on their necks, but sticking it would guarantee a high score. Luckily, Karmakar stuck her landing and survived the vault of death, but she was no match for the high-flying powerhouse from Texas. Simone Biles completed her two difficult vaults and won the gold. Her performance on the balance beam didn't go quite as well. She was forced to grab the beam once to prevent a fall, pushing her into position for the bronze, but Simone was happy to see her teammate Laurie Hernandez walk away with the silver.

When the floor routine rolled around once again, Simone was ready, and so was the crowd. The cheers were deafening.

Quotes About Simone Biles

"She's a special athlete, very unique with a God-given talent that you don't teach. Her coach, Aimee, is great in improving upon that, but it's something that she was born with."

—Retired American gymnast and 1984 Olympian Mary Lou Retton

"Her comments, her performance, I feel like she's 35 years old, mentally. She's just so incredible. If anything, I wish I could be like her when I was younger."

—American tennis player Serena Williams

"Simone is an amazing Olympic champion and I am a big fan. However, only time will tell if she will become the greatest of all time."

—Retired Romanian gymnast and five-time Olympic gold medalist Nadia Comăneci

"I just have to say Simone Biles is truly my little hero; she is amazing, she is the best gymnast that I have ever seen out there. And I would never think that a female or a male gymnast would be doing the spectacular gymnastics that she is doing today."

—Retired American gymnast and 1996 Olympian Dominique Dawes

"I've seen Simone Biles grow as a person and gymnast over the past several years, and what is perhaps most impressive of all is Simone's genuine, kind-hearted spirit and love of life."

—Retired American gymnast and 1996 Olympian Dominique Moceanu

"Learning the rules is tricky, but not nearly as tricky as, say, learning to do 'the Biles'—that crazy move Simone does when she follows two backflips with a half twist."

—American gymnast, 2016 Olympian, and teammate Laurie Hernandez

"[Simone's] honesty impressed me almost as much as her energy … We had texted before we met in person, and years later she showed me a video someone had taken of her reaction when I texted her the first time. She screamed, fell on the ground, and was her typically hyper self."

—American gymnast, 2012 and 2016 Olympian, and teammate Aly Raisman

Gold medalist Simone Biles and silver medalist Aly Raisman are shown here after the all-around competition of the 2016 Olympics.

With the world cheering her on, Simone Biles performed her floor routine with confidence. Standing on the podium with the gold medal around her neck, she felt a little sad. For years, she had been preparing for this moment, to compete in the Olympics. Now, it was over! However, under that twinge of melancholy and the feeling of the competition stress melting away, Simone Biles knew that she was now the most decorated gymnast in the world. She did what she had wanted to do so long ago, looking up at a trampoline in longing.

Zac Efron Fulfills a Fan's Wish

In an interview on *The Ellen DeGeneres Show*, Simone Biles broke into a fit of giggles when Ellen brought up her rumored crush on actor Zac Efron. Ellen even presented Simone with a custom leotard covered with photographs of her crush. In a later interview with NBC's Hoda Kotb, Simone admitted she even had a cardboard cutout of the actor at home. When Kotb asked how Simone would feel if Efron came to see her perform in Rio, she replied that she would "pass out." The two eventually talked on Twitter when Efron tagged Simone in a comment congratulating her on making it to the finals. With some help from Kotb, Efron finally hopped a plane to Brazil to meet his number-one fan. As the United States team walked into the room to be interviewed by Kotb, Efron stepped out of hiding and surprised them.

"He's even more gorgeous in person!" said Simone. She had another surprise when she discovered that Team USA had voted for Simone to carry the flag in the closing ceremonies. With more than one dream fulfilled at last, Simone Biles headed back to the United States.

Coca-Cola
Coca-Cola

Chapter 5

Simone Carries On

After the Olympics drew to a close, Simone Biles was ready for a nice, long, relaxing break, but things weren't going to settle down quite yet. First, at the end of August, Aimee Boorman announced that she would be leaving her position at the World Champions Centre and taking the job of executive director of women's gymnastics at Evo Athletics in Sarasota, Florida. This would mean leaving coaching Simone as well. Simone was sad to see her former coach go, but both felt glad to move on to the next step in their lives. Aimee was sure to remind Simone that she was always around if her former student needed her.

Then, in September, Russian hackers gained access to Simone's private medical records and posted them online, hoping that her use of Ritalin, an ADHD medication, was in violation of anti-doping regulations. These regulations prohibit illegal doping, which includes the use of steroids and growth hormones, to improve an athlete's performance. However, USA Gymnastics had approved Simone's use of the drug, so she knew that she hadn't violated any

Opposite: Back in the United States, Simone celebrated her wins by making public appearances. Here, she showed up at the Chicago Blackhawks versus St. Louis Blues hockey game.

rules. Still, she was upset that there was a stigma surrounding taking medication for ADHD. "Having ADHD, and taking medicine for it is nothing to be ashamed of nothing that I'm afraid to let people know," she posted on Twitter in response to the criticism. This controversy ultimately educated the public on the myths surrounding ADHD and the use of Ritalin to treat it. "[ADHD drugs like Ritalin] simply level the playing field so that someone like Simone Biles has the same amount of dopamine in her prefrontal cortex as her competitors do," said Dr. Ronald Kamm, former president of the International Society for Sports Psychiatry in an interview with ESPN.

Coaches working with athletes with untreated ADHD often bench players who seem scatterbrained or hyperactive, both potential characteristics of ADHD. With Simone bringing this disorder into the spotlight, it helped to shed light on ADHD itself and helped to educate coaches on changing how they work with players dealing with behavioral disorders.

This controversy wasn't the last one that would put Simone Biles in the spotlight at the end of 2016. The United States women's gymnastics program was getting ready to face one of the biggest scandals in its history.

Gymnastics and the Lasting Impact of Abuse

In August 2016, a former gymnast named Rachael Denhollander sent an email to a reporter at the *Indianapolis Star*, alleging that she had been the victim of sexual abuse in the early 2000s at the hands of USA Gymnastics and Michigan State University team physician Larry Nassar. Denhollander was fifteen at the time of the abuse

Former gymnast Rachael Denhollander appears in court in January 2018 to give her victim impact statement during Larry Nassar's sentencing.

and had been experiencing lower back pain, for which she sought help from Nassar. For years, Denhollander, who eventually became an attorney, had been building up a case file against the doctor and working toward bringing her accusations to light in a way she knew simply couldn't be ignored. When women come forward with allegations of sexual abuse or assault, they're often dismissed by police and other officials if there isn't a witness to corroborate the claim. Therefore, Rachael Denhollander knew she had to be prepared and that she would be totally alone as the first woman to stand up and accuse Nassar of abuse. However, she wouldn't be alone for long. Former Olympic gymnast Jamie Dantzscher would soon come forward with her own stories of abuse by Nassar. More former gymnasts came forward. The list of victims grew from a few to almost two hundred, with Simone Biles adding her name to the list in early 2018. "For too long I've asked myself, 'Was I too naive? Was it my fault?' I now know the answer to those questions," she said in a statement at the time.

With so many former and active American gymnasts coming forward, many asked if Nassar's abuse had really gone unnoticed by Bela and Martha Karolyi. In 2017, Mattie Larson, a gymnast who had once trained at Karolyi Ranch, filed a civil suit against the Karolyis for ignoring complaints of the abuse. Former elite gymnast Sabrina Vega filed her own suit in May 2018. The Karolyis denied any wrongdoing, but USA Gymnastics decided to cut ties with the Karolyi Ranch, which had for three decades been the hub of elite gymnastics training.

Other evidence soon came to light, proving that USA Gymnastics (USAG) and the United States Olympic Committee (USOC) had also received reports of sexual abuse dating back to 1999 and didn't take action. As a result, the entire USAG board was forced to resign their posts.

Found guilty in February 2018 of sexual assault, Nassar was sentenced to up to 175 years in prison. Simone's teammate and friend Aly Raisman appeared at the sentencing and read her own statement regarding her experiences of abuse by Nassar, which started when she was fifteen.

The Karolyis filed a lawsuit in May 2018 against USAG and the USOC seeking damages after the sale of Karolyi Ranch fell through. They felt that they were not responsible for Larry Nassar's actions. Their suit is still pending as of summer 2019.

The accusations against Nassar opened up discussions about other types of abuse. Gymnasts came forward with stories about how they were treated at the Karolyi Ranch, saying that the Karolyis often used verbal abuse to get results from their athletes. Many gymnasts were denied food or forced to train or compete with sometimes severe injuries, like broken bones. Former Romanian gymnasts added accusations of physical abuse by the Karolyis.

This brought about a much bigger conversation concerning American gymnastics and the pressure felt by gymnasts to win in competitions. Elite gymnasts often deal with debilitating injuries that impact the rest of their lives, sometimes requiring more than one surgery. They sometimes suffer from stress-induced anxiety and eating disorders that don't go away after they retire.

Many wonder if the pressure to win medals for Team USA has become more important than the safety of the athletes. This issue will continue to have a big impact on women's gymnastics going into the 2020 Olympics and beyond. The most important thing for many gymnasts, though, is that they've finally found the courage to speak out against some of the toxic culture in their sport.

Making a Difference

Simone Biles got to enjoy lots of amazing new experiences during her hiatus from gymnastics. In late 2016, she partnered with the Kids Wish Network, an organization that grants wishes for sick

Simone continued to stay in the spotlight long after the 2016 Olympics were over.

kids. Late that year, Simone, along with Aly Raisman and American gymnast Shawn Johnson, met Melinda Ortega, a former gymnastics hopeful whose training was cut short by a diagnosis of juvenile dermatomyositis. Ortega was picked up by a limousine and brought to the Wells Fargo training center to meet some of her heroes.

In May 2017, Simone competed on ABC's *Dancing with the Stars*. She came in fourth place with partner Sasha Farber. "It's ok," she said after her elimination from the competition. "I'm just thankful to be at this competition. I feel like I've learned a lot about myself. I've matured. And I can't wait to go home!"

Simone also took some time to talk to kids about staying active and healthy at a Triple Play Day event in July 2017, in Washington, DC. The event was created by the Boys and Girls Clubs of America and encouraged play and exercise for children.

Simone also used her downtime to help out in a crisis. In August 2017, Houston was hit by Hurricane Harvey, a Category 4 hurricane with winds up to 130 miles per hour (209.2 kilometers per hour) when it made landfall. Over the next three days, 27 trillion gallons (102.2 trillion liters) of rain fell on Texas.

In Houston, thousands of people were left homeless because of the flooding. Lots of athletes and celebrities showed up to help, volunteering at shelters and helping to collect donations. Simone Biles was right alongside all of them, helping out as much as she could and urging others to help as well. "There is always something you can do to give back & it doesn't always have to be money," she said to fans via Twitter.

Simone also made some big changes in her personal life. During her hiatus, she moved into her own apartment and started dating fellow gymnast Stacey Ervin.

Simone's Big Comeback

By 2018, Simone was ready to get back to gymnastics. Coming back after a hiatus requires a lot of time at the gym, retraining the body to perform amazing feats again. Simone also needed to consider if her body could handle the pressure. She turned twenty-one in 2018, making her older than a lot of her competition. She hired a new coach, Laurent Landi, Madison Kocian's former coach and a former gymnast himself. Simone felt good about her choice. "He does a good job not letting pressure get to the athletes. You can see some coaches get stressed but he doesn't," she said in an interview with the *Houston Chronicle.*

Simone's first competition of her comeback was the United States Classic in July. Before the competition, reporters asked her to compare 2016 Simone Biles to 2018 Simone Biles: Who was better? Simone confidently replied that she would be at her best in 2018, and she was.

Simone took the gold in the all-around competition, floor exercise, vault, and balance beam. After a mistake on the uneven bars, she dropped to the floor briefly, but she got back up and finished strong with her dismount. She ended up with a score of 15.2.

In August, at the second meet of her comeback—the USA Gymnastics National Championships—Simone won every gold medal. She swept all four individual events and the all-around. The last gymnast to do this was Dominique Dawes in 1994. Additionally, to help raise awareness about sexual abuse, Simone wore a special teal leotard. Teal is the color of sexual assault awareness.

The World Championships took place in November 2018 in Qatar, and Simone was ready—well, almost ready. The night before qualifications, Simone took a trip to the emergency room suffering from pain caused by a kidney stone. A kidney stone is a hard deposit formed from minerals and salts inside the kidney. When the buildup becomes large, it can be extremely painful. Discovering that treatment for the stone would definitely take her out of the competition, Simone decided to just deal with the pain and delay treating it.

During the competition, she came in first in the all-around, floor exercise, vault, and balance beam. She won the silver for the uneven bars. She even debuted a brand-new vault. The new vault is a variation of the Cheng but with an extra half twist added so that she lands it facing forward in a blind landing. All of this was accomplished while dealing with a kidney stone. After that competition, Simone had officially won twenty World Championship medals. The only other gymnast to do that is Svetlana Khorkina of Russia.

On March 16, 2019, Simone won the all-around title at the World Cup held in Stuttgart, Germany. Her impressive score of 58.8 points was 3.5 points higher than Ana Padurariu of Canada.

What's Next?

After that kind of success, one might expect Simone Biles to retire, but that doesn't seem to be in the cards as of 2019. She's enjoying her success on and off the gymnastics mat. She's a strong brand ambassador for Nike, Kellogg's, and other major companies.

Simone Biles Scorecard

Career Highlights: Named AT&T American Cup silver medalist (2013); won all-around and vault gold medal at US Championships (2013); won two gold medals at the World Championships in all-around and floor exercise (2013); won US Championships gold for all-around, floor exercise, and vault (2014); won four gold medals for team, all-around, balance beam, and floor exercise at Worlds (2014); won gold medals for all-around, vault, and balance beam at US Championships (2015); celebrated third consecutive gold medal for all-around competition at Worlds, also winning gold for team, balance beam, and floor exercise (2015); became Pacific Rim Championship team and all-around champion gold medalist (2016); won gold in all-around, vault, balance beam, and floor exercise at US Championships (2016); won five Olympic medals, including four gold for team, all-around, vault, and floor exercise (2016); won gold for all-around, vault, and floor exercise at World Championships (2018); won all-around at Stuttgart World Cup (2019).

Firsts: First to win four gold medals at a single World Championships (2014) since the Soviet Union's Ludmilla Tourischeva did it in 1974; first to tie Olympic record for most medals won (four) by a female gymnast in a single Olympic Games (2016); first to win fourteen gold medals at World Championships; first to be declared most decorated US women's gymnast of all time with 25 World/Olympic medals.

Honors: Named Women's Sports Foundation individual Sportswoman of the Year (2014); named ESPN's Woman of the Year (2016); became Associated Press Female Athlete of the Year (2016); named Most Dominant Athlete by *ESPN* magazine (2018); honored with Laureus Sportswoman of the Year (2018); named Houston Sports Athlete of the Year (2018).

Teal has long been considered the color of bringing awareness to issues of sexual violence. Here, Simone appears in her teal leotard, worn in solidarity with Larry Nassar's other victims.

"Simone Biles' net worth is going to continue to grow—and we honestly can't think of anyone more deserving of the big bucks," said chief strategy officer of Wunderman New York Nelson Freitas to Refinery29 in 2016.

Not only that, Simone continues to influence young gymnasts around the world who just want to fly high like their idol. "I remember going to meets as a kid, like the Mary Lou Retton invitational," said Simone Biles in 2017. "Once I won, I got first place, she crowned me, so that was a super exciting moment for me. I'll always remember that. Hopefully I'll do the same with those kids, and get to interact with them."

Timeline

July 1996 The Magnificent Seven women's gymnastics team wins gold in the team finals at the Olympics in Atlanta, Georgia.

March 14, 1997 Simone Arianne Biles is born in Columbus, Ohio.

2003 Biles begins training in gymnastics at Bannon's Gymnastix.

November 7, 2003 Simone and her sister Adria are adopted officially by Ron and Nellie Biles.

2007 Biles begins competing as a level eight gymnast.

2008 Biles earns the highest all-around score at the South Padre Invitational Meet.

2010 Biles enjoys her first level ten win at the Houston National Invitational.

July 2011 Biles competes in the American Classic at the age of fourteen.

August 2011 Biles has a disastrous performance at the 2011 Visa National Championships.

June 2012 Biles is named to the women's junior national team.

July 2012 The Fierce Five women's gymnastics team wins gold at the Olympics held in London.

July 2013 An exhausted Biles performs poorly at the US Secret Classic.

September 2013 Biles competes in her first World Championships, winning golds for the all-around event and floor.

August 2014 Biles wins her second all-around title at the P&G National Championships.

October 2014 Biles wins her second all-around gold medal at the World Championships.

November 1, 2015 Biles wins a third gold medal for the all-around at the World Championships.

April 2016 Biles debuts her Cheng vault at the Pacific Rim Championships.

July 2016 Biles places first at Olympic team trials.

August 2016 Biles competes in her first Olympic games, winning gold in the team, all-around, floor, and vault.

2016–2017 Accusations against team physician Larry Nassar surface.

2018 Biles wins a fourth gold medal for the all-around at Worlds.

March 16, 2019 Biles wins the all-around title at the World Cup held in Stuttgart, Germany.

Glossary

all-around A gymnastics event where gymnasts are scored by performances on all four apparatuses.

Amanar A type of vault that begins with a roundoff onto the springboard, followed by a back handspring onto the platform, and then a two-and-a-half-twist flip onto the mat.

artistic gymnastics The type of gymnastics where gymnasts train in and perform four individual events.

attention-deficit/hyperactivity disorder (ADHD) A behavioral disorder characterized by difficulty paying attention, trouble controlling certain behaviors, and hyperactivity.

balance beam A gymnastics apparatus consisting of a narrow plank held up off the floor, requiring athletes to maintain strict balance during stunts.

burnout A state of overwhelming exhaustion (physical, mental, or emotional) as a result of long-term, intense stress.

Cheng A vault consisting of a roundoff onto the board, followed by a half turn onto the platform, followed by a Rudi.

elite gymnast A gymnast who has trained and competes at the highest level.

floor exercise A type of choreographed gymnastics performed on a springy mat; it features "passes" or sequences of tumbling skills performed from one corner of the mat to the opposite one.

foam pit A pit filled with foam cubes that allows an inexperienced gymnast to fall and practice without risk of injury.

giant A skill in which a gymnast rotates 360 degrees around the bar with her body fully extended.

handspring A maneuver in which a gymnast flips forward onto her hands and then "springs" back onto her feet using her arms, doing a complete rotation of the body.

homeschool A system of education in which a student learns at home, taught either by a parent or accredited teacher.

Junior Olympic program A program through which gymnasts achieve "levels" based on age and difficulty, created in order to prevent injury.

layout A flip performed with the body fully extended; a twist can be added for extra flair.

leotard A one-piece garment worn by gymnasts that offers maximum movement for arms and legs; often made in bright colors or with sequins added for style.

Produnova A vault that consists of a front handspring onto the platform followed by two front somersaults in a tucked position; often called the "vault of death."

qualifier A competition before a larger event wherein the top scorers can move on to the next stage of the competition.

recreational gymnastics Fun, noncompetitive gymnastics programs where tumblers can learn new acrobatic skills.

straddle back A maneuver on the uneven bars in which a gymnast launches herself backward in a straddle from the high bar to the low bar, catching the low bar in a handstand.

Tkatchev A maneuver on the bars in which a gymnast gains speed performing a giant and then releases the bar, flies backward over the top of it, and catches it again.

uneven bars A gymnastics apparatus composed of a steel frame with two bars, one high and one low, upon which a gymnast performs a variety of stunts, moving seamlessly between the bars.

vault A gymnastics apparatus composed of a springboard and a platform; gymnasts run toward it, use the springboard to leap onto the platform, and then perform an aerial stunt pushing off from the platform, before landing back on the mat.

Further Information

Books

Biles, Simone. *Courage to Soar: A Body in Motion, a Life in Balance.* New York, NY: HarperCollins, 2016.

Meyers, Dvora. *The End of the Perfect 10: The Making and Breaking of Gymnastics' Top Score—from Nadia to Now*. New York, NY: Atria Books, 2017.

Raisman, Aly. *Fierce: How Competing for Myself Changed Everything.* New York, NY: Little, Brown and Company, 2017.

Websites

NBC Olympics: Gymnastics

https://www.nbcolympics.com/gymnastics/
The NBC Olympics website provides information about the sport of gymnastics.

Olympic Games

https://www.olympic.org/international-gymnastics-federation
The Olympic Games official website is a good resource for learning more about the different gymnastics events.

Simone Biles

http://www.simonebiles.com
This is the official website of Simone Biles. It features a biography, as well as information about her book, sponsors, and social media posts.

USA Gymnastics

https://usagym.org
The website for USA Gymnastics is a great place for learning more about different events and competitions and how to get more involved in the sport.

World Champions Centre

https://www.worldchampionscentre.com
The World Champions Centre in Spring, Texas, is a gymnastics gym owned and operated by Ron and Nellie Biles, Simone Biles's parents.

Videos

2011 United States Junior Nationals

https://www.youtube.com/watch?v=73spBTH3rQg
See Simone Biles perform in 2011, at the age of thirteen, before she became the champion she is today.

2018 World Championships

https://www.youtube.com/watch?v=t47N9TZYbck
Watch Simone Biles in action, performing her floor routine at the World Championships in 2018.

Bibliography

Barron, David. "Simone Biles Ready to Speak to Investigators About Abuse at Karolyi Ranch." *Houston Chronicle*, January 31, 2018. https://www.houstonchronicle.com/olympics/article/Simone-Biles-ready-to-speak-to-investigators-12541069.php.

Bastién, Angelica Jade. "Why the Women's Gymnastics Team's Greatness Is Revolutionary." *Rolling Stone*, August 5, 2016. https://www.rollingstone.com/culture/culture-sports/why-the-womens-gymnastics-teams-greatness-is-revolutionary-249786/.

Biles, Simone. *Courage to Soar: A Body in Motion, A Life in Balance*. New York, NY: HarperCollins, 2016.

Brady, James. "Olympic Trials 2016, Women's Gymnastic Results: Simone Biles Leads After Day 1." SB Nation, July 8, 2016. https://www.sbnation.com/2016/7/8/12133972/olympics-trials-2016-womens-gymnastics-results-simone-biles.

Brody, Liz. "The Army of Women Who Took Down Larry Nassar." *Glamour*, October 30, 2018. https://www.glamour.com/story/women-of-the-year-2018-larry-nassar-survivors.

Connor, Tracy. "Simone Biles Says She Was Molested by Gymnastics Doctor Larry Nassar." NBC News, January 15, 2018. https://www.nbcnews.com/news/us-news/simone-biles-says-she-was-molested-gymnastics-doctor-larry-nassar-n837806.

Crawford, Aimee. "Bravo, Simone Biles, for Taking a Stand Against ADHD Stigma." ESPN, September 21, 2016. http://www.espn.com/espnw/voices/article/17602540/bravo-simone-biles-taking-stand-adhd-stigma.

Dzidrums, Christine. *Simone Biles: Superstar of Gymnastics.* Whittier, CA: Creative Media, Inc., 2016.

Evans, Kelley D. "Dominique Dawes Talks Simone Biles, Family and Courage." The Undefeated, August 29, 2016. http://theundefeated.com/features/dominique-dawes-talks-simone-biles-family-and-courage/.

Fitzgerald, Katherine. "Olympic Star Simone Biles Leads Campaign to Encourage Kids to Live Healthy." *USA Today,* July 20, 2017. https://www.usatoday.com/story/sports/olympics/2017/07/20/olympic-star-simone-biles-encourage-kids-live-healthy/497746001/.

Gilmer, Marcus. "This Chart Shows Just How High Simone Biles Can Jump." Mashable, August 17, 2016. https://mashable.com/2016/08/17/how-high-does-simone-biles-jump/#LNKEphXr78qk.

Gilroy, Rosie Holden Vacanti. "What Is the Amanar Vault? There's a Long Story Behind This Famous US Gymnastics Move." Bustle, August 4, 2016. https://www.bustle.com/articles/176815-what-is-the-amanar-vault-theres-a-long-story-behind-this-famous-us-gymnastics-move.

Graves, Will. "'Fierce Five' Soar Their Way into Olympic History." *Seattle Times,* July 31, 2012. https://www.seattletimes.com/sports/fierce-five-soar-their-way-into-olympic-history/.

Gray, Danielle. "Simone Biles Responds to Internet Haters Criticizing Her Hair." *Allure,* December 13, 2017. https://www.allure.com/story/simone-biles-hair-criticism-clapback.

Harrison, Olivia. "This Is How Much Simone Biles' Endorsement Deals Are Worth—& That's Expected to Keep Growing." Refinery29, August 18, 2016. https://www.refinery29.com/en-us/2016/08/120531/simone-biles-endorsement-deals.

Jerkins, Morgan. "The Unconventional Legacy of Dominique Dawes." The Undefeated, July 22, 2016. https://theundefeated.com/features/the-unconventional-legacy-of-dominique-dawes/.

Kids Wish Network. "Kids Wish Network Partners with U.S. Olympic Women's Gymnastics Team to Grant a Once-in-a-Lifetime Experience for Chicago Wish Kid." Kids Wish Network, November 2016. https://www.kidswishnetwork.org/2016/11/kids-wish-network-partners-with-u-s-olympic-womens-gymnastics-team-to-grant-a-once-in-a-lifetime-experience-for-chicago-wish-kid/.

Krishnamurthy, Madhu. "Mary Lou Retton on Being 'America's Sweetheart,' Retiring at 18." *Daily Herald*, October 11, 2016. https://www.dailyherald.com/article/20161011/news/161019757/.

Lasher, Megan. "Serena Williams Wishes She Could Have Been Like Simone Biles." *TIME*, October 5, 2016. http://time.com/4519526/serena-williams-simone-biles/.

Lawrence, Blythe. "Simone Biles (Easily) Wins All-Around at Stuttgart World Cup, Her First Meet of 2019." Team USA, March 17, 2019. https://www.teamusa.org/News/2019/March/17/Simone-Biles-Easily-Wins-All-Around-At-Stuttgart-World-Cup-Her-First-Meet-Of-2019.

Mather, Victor. "U.S.A. Gymnastics Cuts Ties with Karolyi Ranch Training Center." *New York Times*, January 18, 2018. https://www.nytimes.com/2018/01/18/sports/usa-gymnastics-karolyi-ranch.html.

Miller, Korin. "Simone Biles Went to the ER with a Kidney Stone—and Made It to the World Championship Finals the Next Day." *Self*, October 29, 2018. https://www.self.com/story/simone-biles-kidney-stone-world-championships-finals.

Minutaglio, Rose. "1984 Olympic Gold Medalist Mary Lou Retton Says Simone Biles 'Is the Greatest Gymnast Ever.'" *People*, August 16, 2016. https://people.com/sports/mary-lou-retton-calls-simone-biles-greatest-gymnast-ever/.

Minutaglio, Rose. "Simone Biles Parts Ways with Trainer Who Coached Her Since She Was 8 Years Old." *People*, August 29, 2016. https://people.com/sports/simone-biles-splits-from-longtime-coach-aimee-boorman/.

NPR. "How He Got Caught." NPR, November 19, 2018. https://www.npr.org/2018/11/16/668629660/how-he-got-caught.

O'Neal, Lonnae. "The Difficulty of Being Simone Biles." The Undefeated, July 6, 2016. https://theundefeated.com/features/the-difficulty-of-being-simone-biles/.

Papenfuss, Mary. "Simone Biles Rips New Gymnastics Chief for Nike Attack After Colin Kaepernick Ad." *Huffington Post*, October 15, 2018. https://www.huffingtonpost.com/entry/simone-biles-rips-new-gymnastics-head-mary-bono-for-attack-on-nike_us_5bc3dba4e4b0bd9ed55b6977.

Park, Alice. "Why It's a Big Deal That USA Gymnastics Is Cutting Ties with the Karolyi Ranch." *TIME*, January 18, 2018. http://time.com/5108887/usa-gymnastics-sexual-abuse-karolyi-ranch/.

Pathi, Krutika. "How Is a Gymnastics Team Captain Chosen? The Process Is More Straightforward Than You Think." Bustle, August 9, 2016. https://www.bustle.com/articles/177838-how-is-a-gymnastics-team-captain-chosen-the-process-is-more-straightforward-than-you-think.

Stump, Scott. "Watch Simone Biles Nearly Pass Out When Crush Zac Efron Surprises Her in Rio." *Today,* August 17, 2016. https://www.today.com/popculture/watch-simone-biles-nearly-pass-out-when-crush-zac-efron-t101922.

Van Deusen, Amy. "The Hardest Skills in Women's Gymnastics." ThoughtCo, July 9, 2018. https://www.thoughtco.com/hardest-skills-in-womens-gymnastics-1714810.

Vora, Shivani. "Why Simone Biles Loves Belize." *New York Times,* September 16, 2016. https://www.nytimes.com/2016/09/18/travel/why-simone-biles-loves-belize.html.

Weiss, Mitch, and Holbrook Mohr. "U.S. Gymnasts Say Sport Rife with Verbal and Emotional Abuse." *Chicago Tribune,* February 23, 2018. https://www.chicagotribune.com/sports/international/ct-us-gymnasts-verbal-emotional-abuse-20180223-story.html.

WITW Staff. "Olympic Committee Knew About Sexual Abuse in Gymnastics Since the 1990s, According to Court Filings." Women in the World, November 26, 2018. https://womenintheworld.com/2018/11/26/olympic-committee-knew-about-sexual-abuse-in-gymnastics-since-the-1990s-according-to-court-filings/.

Zaccardi, Nick. "Simone Biles Wins Every Gold Medal at U.S. Championships." NBC News, August 19, 2018. https://olympics.nbcsports.com/2018/08/19/simone-biles-wins-gymnastics-national-championships/.

Index

Page numbers in **boldface** are images.

About the Author

Bethany Bryan is a freelance book editor, specializing in graphic novels for young people, and an author of several books. She enjoys writing biographies, especially ones about famous women who are exciting and driven—women like Simone Biles! Bryan has always loved watching Olympic gymnastics (her favorite of the Magnificent Seven was Shannon Miller), even taking a tumbling class in first grade, but she realized pretty quickly that she would never master a basic handstand. She can still, however, do a cartwheel and admires anyone who can catch a Tkatchev on the high bar or perform an Amanar and stick the landing. Bryan lives in Kansas City, Missouri.